A DAY AT THE ROMAN GAMES

TOBY FORWARD ILLUSTRATED BY STEVE NOON

ORDER of EVENTS

The Arrival of the Emperor
The Great Hunt
The Animal Fights
The Execution of Criminals
The Gladiatorial Contests

CANDLEWICK PRESS

MARCUS WAS AFRAID,

and he hated himself for it. All his life he had longed to get to Rome, and now as he looked down on the city for the first time, he felt frightened. It wasn't the city itself that frightened Marcus. Since he and his fellow herdsmen had been captured eight years ago, he had seen many great cities. But none as big as Rome. He had lived in Carthage, that great port on the coast of Africa where people lived as the Romans did, with baths and great villas, fountains and public squares. He had seen great ships dock and load and unload cargo. He remembered with shame what it felt like to be cargo himself: a slave, the property of the beast master who had bought him when he was four years old. He was almost a man now. As he sat in the darkness outside Rome itself, he could see the vastness of the city spread before him. And dominating it all was the great Colosseum.

Marcus stared at it and felt his heart quicken, his breathing grow short, and the skin on his back tingle. He knew what was to happen there later today, and although he was too young to fight there now, one day he might. He feared it, and he longed for it, for this was the place where he could one day win his freedom. Of course, Timon would fight today, and, as ever, he might return victorious. Or he might not return at all.

Marcus thought of Timon as a father. Like Marcus, Timon was a slave, but from one of the barbarian nations of the north, Dacia. He too had been captured, in battle, and had been brought back to Rome in disgrace, led through the streets, chained and shackled with hundreds of others. Timon was lucky. He had been sold—unlike others who were killed in the celebrations or put into the arena for entertainment, where they faced a painful death. He was bought by Quintus, a beast master, and taken to Africa the next day.

THE CITY OF ROME

The streets of Rome were always busy with people trading goods and socializing.

The main buildings for government, religious ceremonies, and entertainment (like the Colosseum and the public baths) were in the center of town, around the Forum—an open area like a town square.

Rich people lived in large villas with painted walls, mosaic floors, and gardens, but poor Roman citizens lived in apartment buildings up to five or six stories high. They were often badly constructed, increasing the risk of fire. Many of these apartments overlooked narrow streets lined with shops and taverns. It would have been easy to get lost in Rome, since none of the streets were named.

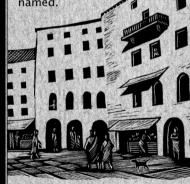

Timon was superb with animals. He had worked with horses before he became a soldier, and during the campaigns he had tended the army horses. Quintus paid a high price for Timon, but the beast master had been repaid many times over in the lives of the animals Timon looked after. All beast masters lost animals on their way to the arena; it was part of the profit and loss of the business. But Quintus lost fewer beasts than anyone, because of Timon.

Timon not only tended the animals for Quintus. He was also one of the most powerful gladiators and earned good money for his master performing at events in the arena. Marcus dreaded these events, and the thought of losing Timon was more than he could bear.

Marcus dragged his thoughts away from Timon and turned his eyes to the huge oval of the Colosseum. He tried to picture the events to come later that day, but as he looked, his eyelids drooped and he fell asleep.

|||||||||||||||||||||||||||||||||

LUCIUS HAD HEARD

the calls of the wild animals night after night as their cries drifted in through his bedroom window on the breeze.

When the Games had first begun, the sounds had sometimes woken him. Then he had slept through them. The deep roars of the tigers and the squeals and calls of the other beasts became part of the background of his sleep.

Tonight a new sound had broken through the cool, starlit air: a fanfare, like a trumpet. At first, it entered his sleep as part of his dream. Then, suddenly, he was sitting up in bed, wide awake. The sky outside was still dark, and the room was empty, but he could still hear the fanfare—that same single, sad note over and over. He made his way to the window, looked out, and listened. The noise was coming from the direction of the countryside outside the walls, mingling with the noises of the other animals. Were they playing music to the animals? Why?

Lucius returned to bed and lay looking up into the darkness until it folded him back into sleep, the melancholy music still in his ears.

MARCUS WAS COLD when Timon found him. He woke the boy gently and put his cloak around him. He and the boy were close. When Marcus had first arrived, a tiny, crying four-year-old, he would not eat and kicked anyone who came near him. Quintus had bought him cheap—no one else would take him—and the beast master knew a boy would always be useful for feeding the animals and doing the dirty jobs a man resented. But at first it seemed Marcus wasn't worth the few coins Quintus had paid. He was more like a wild animal himself than a person.

Timon had seen that Marcus was ill with grief for his lost parents. Saying nothing, Timon took him and put him in the horses' quarters. Safe on the straw, away from the horses' swift hooves, Marcus watched with quick, frightened eyes as the big man groomed his charges. He listened to Timon's soothing murmuring. He saw him feed the animals and give them water before he took refreshment himself. And when Timon did sit to eat, he settled himself close to Marcus, with the food between them. Over time, Marcus began to eat and drink with Timon: a little at first, then more. When tiredness came over Marcus and he began to sleep, Timon would draw him close, put a thick arm around him, stroke his hair, and make the same low, gentle noise the horses liked.

For weeks they lived like this. Marcus grew calm, and the hollows in his cheeks disappeared, but he never spoke. Sometimes he would stand very close to Timon as he groomed the horses, and once he left the stables with him to watch him work with the other animals: the tigers, the gazelles, the ostriches, the zebras, the baboons.

As they worked more and more together, Marcus began to talk. He told Timon all he could remember of his life in the desert, and Timon told Marcus a little about his life in the north country, his family, the farm he had lived on, and the horses and animals he had owned and cared for there. Marcus saw how skillfully Timon handled the animals and quickly learned how to look after them himself.

Timon watched over Marcus and always looked for him when he was missing. So it was Timon who discovered Marcus asleep above the city.

"We need to get started," he said. "Quintus is awake."

Marcus scrambled to his feet, and together they set off down the hill toward the camp. It didn't take them long, but when they arrived, Quintus had already started his breakfast—a bowl of puls. He was in high spirits and began chatting

ROMAN FOOD

Wealthy Roman citizens usually ate three meals a day: a small breakfast of bread and fruit, a light midday meal, and dinner in the evening.

These rich Romans liked to show off their wealth by holding dinner parties. The food was expensive and difficult to make, which was more important to the Romans than whether it tasted good. The dinner parties took place in highly decorated dining rooms where the guests would recline on sofas, resting on their left elbows, leaving their right hands free to pick at the food.

Depending on how wealthy the host was, a guest might feast on dormice dipped in honey, flamingo or parrot, and even whole plates of peacock tongues. The main drink was wine diluted with water.

Poor people were much more restricted in their diet and had to eat cheaper foods. Puls, a porridge made from barley, was a staple, as were eggs and cheese. They would have eaten very little meat.

merrily with Timon about his prospects for the day.

Marcus had been so sleepy on the way back to camp, he realized he'd forgotten to ask Timon an important question. Seeing Quintus distracted for a moment, Marcus leaned toward his friend. "Do you think it will be today?" he whispered.

Timon shook his head. "Never mention it," he said.

Every time a gladiator fought in front of the emperor, there was a chance he would walk into the arena a slave and walk out a free man. And there was every chance he would die. It was all at the mercy of the gods. Marcus looked at his friend swallowing his puls and arguing with Quintus. Timon was all the family he had. He didn't want to lose him.

Marcus chewed a piece of bread and half-closed his eyes, drifting into a waking dream of a home he had never known. Suddenly he was roused by coarse laughter nearby. The stars of the arena, the great gladiators, were shouting jokes to one another about how they would triumph in the Colosseum later that day. They were called Salvus, Porcinus, Globus, and Aquillus. They'd had other names once, real names, but no one could remember them now. Their nicknames had become their real names.

These four gladiators were tough. Aquillus and Porcinus were retiarii, Salvus was a mirmillo, and Globus, a gigantic hoplomachus.

All were battle-scarred, but they were lucky even to be alive after so many fights. One trick to their survival was that they tried to make sure never to fight one another.

GLADIATORS

HOPLOMACHUS

The word hoplomachus
means "armed fighter."
These gladiators wore
heavy armor and used
shields and spears
as weapons.

RETIARIUS

This type of gladiator
wore a light tunic and
fought with a net and
a trident.

MIRMILLO

A mirmillo was a heavily
armed gladiator who held
a rectangular shield
and wore a
visored helmet with a
fish-shaped crest.

It was a cunning tactic, not easy to manage, but it had saved their lives many times.

Seeing Marcus staring at him, Porcinus caught the boy's eye and yelled to Quintus, "When's that boy going to fight with us?"

Everyone burst out laughing at the joke, but Timon glared at him.

"Give Marcus more breakfast!" Globus joined in. He'd already eaten three bowls of barley and beans.

"He's worth too much to fight," Quintus countered. "Not like you."

The banter continued, and Marcus looked away, embarrassed. He must fight, or he would never be a free man. Death or freedom; one was his future.

॥॥॥॥॥॥॥॥॥॥॥॥॥॥॥॥॥॥॥॥॥॥॥॥॥॥॥

BREAKFAST FOR LUCIUS was a quiet, dignified affair. He was not nervous, but he was so excited that he felt as though he were. Today he would go to the Games for the first time.

Lucius held out his hand, and a slave handed him a hot towel to wipe his fingers clean. No school today, so he was free to do as he wished until it was time to go with his father, Caius, to the Colosseum.

He went first to the atrium, which was filled with people waiting to see his father. Caius was a senator, one of the leaders of Rome. Lucius looked at the line of men, wondering what could make them so unhappy that they had to wait like this to beg his father for help. They seemed poor creatures to him, hardly worth being called Romans at all. When he was a man, he would be a senator too, he thought, but he didn't think he would bother with these creatures. They were little better than slaves.

Just at that moment, Lucius' thoughts were interrupted by a loud trumpeting sound from the city

SENATORS

Ancient Roman senators were like our modern-day politicians. They made laws and made sure everyone did what the emperor wanted. When senators gathered together to discuss politics, they were collectively known as the Senate.

The Senate was made up of about 300 men from Rome's most important (and wealthy) families, although ordinary citizens could elect two people, called consuls, who spoke with the Senate on behalf of the people of Rome.

ORIGINS OF THE GAMES

The first gladiatorial contest in Rome took place in 264 BC. It was a religious ceremony held in memory of a dead Roman merchant and took the form of a fight between two slaves. It soon became popular to hold a contest like this when someone died.

These early contests were held in the Forum and could be watched by any man who was passing by. Over time, seats were added to the makeshift arenas and other entertainments were added. The religious aspect was forgotten, and the games' popularity spread throughout the Roman Empire.

below. He lifted his head in surprise. The fanfare from his dreams! He ran into the street to find the source of the noise, but he saw nothing except a cloud of dust on the hillside, advancing toward Rome—toward the Colosseum.

||||||||||||||||||||||||||||||

"MARCUS! GO AND calm that beast! We mustn't lose him. He's our best money today!" Quintus yelled as the fanfare grew louder and louder. Marcus disappeared silently, and a few seconds later, the trumpeting stopped.

His job done, Marcus looked around to see how the other animals were faring. The wild animals were being rolled along in cages set in wagons. The others, like the gazelles and deer and zebras, whose only job was to run in the arena until they were caught and killed, trotted along in lines. Horses were ridden or led in tethered lines like the others. The ostriches were the worst. They ran all right, but they were more skittish than any other animal, ducking and darting constantly. Their beaks were quick to bite, and their feet could break a man's leg. The crowds loved them. They never won, but they put up a better fight than anything else against the tigers.

It was a short journey, this last leg to the Colosseum, but it was slow and dangerous. Many other beast masters had their animals in place the night before, but Quintus had chosen to spend the final night out of the city. It provided pasture and peace, and more of the animals would survive to enter the arena.

After an hour or so, the dusty track gave way to a finished road, and then, just ahead of Marcus, the wide gates of the Colosseum opened to swallow the whole procession. Marcus was used to arenas, even some of the amphitheaters in the provinces were big. But none could compare to this. The size was astonishing. It seemed to rise up from the ground, growing taller and taller as he approached it, as though swelling to receive him.

The gates through which they entered were not the gates that the emperor and the important men would use but gates that led through low, dark passageways under the arena to a maze of tunnels, cages, and pens. There was shade and there was water here, but there was also the sense of dread and danger.

||||||||||||||||||||||||||||||||||

LUCIUS WANDERED DOWN the crowded street, enjoying the noise and activity, the strange trumpeting noise all but forgotten. The shops were busy. Tradesmen always made a healthy profit on holidays, and Lucius often thought that if he had not been born to be a ruler of Rome, he would have liked to be a shopkeeper. Customers came in, and you showed them your goods: spices, cloth, wine—anything the empire could offer. And when you made some money, you could spend it on something to eat.

Food was never far from the mind of Lucius. Breakfast hardly over, he lingered near a snack stall, sniffing the appetizing aromas coming from the earthenware jars set into the counter, the fires beneath them keeping the food hot. Something spicy and greasy would be nice. There was a particular stallholder who sold the best spicy pastries in Rome, and Lucius decided that he really ought to eat one to celebrate his first visit to the Games. His mind made up, he began to push his way through the crowd.

||||||||||||||||||||||||||||||||

THE VELARIUM

The velarium was an awning that gave shade to the audience in the Colosseum, protecting them from the baking-hot sun. Great sheets of canvas were rigged around the sides of the oval, attached to large poles on the top of the amphitheater. The whole thing was attached to the ground with large ropes. Sailors were specially enlisted from the Roman naval headquarters to work the velarium. It was an expert job. One slip, and they would plunge to their deaths on the stone seats far below.

BACK IN THE COLOSSEUM, MARCUS marveled at the men rigging the awning. He raised his head and shaded his eyes from the sun, trying to follow their movements—they must have been working since dawn.

"Boy! Get back here!" Quintus shouted from the gates. "Go and buy me some food. Something tasty. I don't like the garbage they sell here. And be quick about it." Marcus scampered to him, took the money, and darted past him, back through the maze of tunnels and out into the sunshine of the broad road that ran to the Colosseum. He had spotted a little alley full of shops on the way in that morning. He could even buy himself a treat with Quintus' money. And he would get to explore Rome!

It was all he expected and more: shops the likes of which he had never seen, with so many things to buy! He'd never known the world held such riches. There were many smells: leather, perfume, fruit, and, most important, food.

He found a stall and picked out food that he could carry. Painted on the wall behind the counter were the gods Mercury and Bacchus, to bring prosperity to the stallholder. Mercury was Marcus' own patron, chosen because Mercury was a messenger, as he was. Mercury had wings on his sandals to make him fast. Marcus always wished he had wings too—he had so much to do!

Once Quintus' meal was safely bought, Marcus thought he might spare a few coins for himself. Among the snacks for sale there was one last crescent-shaped spicy pastry on the counter, and Marcus asked the stallholder for it. Just as he

Marcus turned and saw the furious face of a boy about his own age, glaring at him.

"Put that down, slave."

Marcus stared back.

The other boy spoke to the stallholder: "Are there any more of those?"

"That's the last, sir."

Marcus wondered at the stallholder speaking so politely to this rude customer, less than half the man's age.

"Then it's mine, even though this slave has touched it. Put it down," he ordered again.

"I've paid for it," said Marcus. He knew he should never speak like this to a Roman citizen—he could be whipped, at the very least—but he was angry.

"It wasn't a very good one," the stallholder lied. "There will be more and better tomorrow."

"I want it now! Put it down."

"Please let him have it," the stallholder begged Marcus.

"No." Marcus was determined. "Never."

Lucius was white with fury. This could not happen. A slave was nothing. Less then nothing. But short of taking the pastry, there was nothing he could do.

"A slave should never have what a Roman wants," he said.

Marcus thought, then said slowly, "What sort of Roman wants the little a slave can have?" And he held out the pastry.

Lucius was trapped. He didn't want to be seen taking food from a slave, but at the same time, he still wanted the pastry. In the end, his pride conquered his appetite. With a furious glance at Marcus, he turned and stalked off.

The stallholder breathed out, surprised to find that he had been holding his breath. "That was lucky," he said. "And brave, too. You must be the only slave in Rome to take what a citizen wants today. You should enjoy it."

"It isn't for me," said Marcus. He stepped around the counter and crumpled the pastry in front of the painting of Mercury. "Speed to the emperor," he whispered. "Make him give Timon his freedom in the Games today. Please."

The stallholder watched, not hearing the words. "You should have told him," he said to Marcus. "He would not have demanded an offering to the gods."

No," Marcus agreed, "but I wanted him to lose it to a slave."

Quintus was cross at having to wait so long, but with crumbs around his lips and grease trickling into his beard, he congratulated Marcus on his choice of stall. "The best food I've eaten in years," he said.

‖‖‖‖‖‖‖‖‖‖‖‖‖‖‖‖‖‖‖‖‖‖‖‖‖‖‖‖‖

MARCUS KNEW THAT preparation was everything. With only an hour to go, Quintus was pacing up and down like a lion in a cage. Timon had disappeared to prepare for the fight. It was the only time he absolutely forbade Marcus to be with him. However he approached his gods was his secret and not to be shared. The others drank and laughed, as though they could drive away death with ridicule. But it was the animals that showed the tension most. The defenseless animals, who would be torn to pieces first, flared their nostrils and tried helplessly to flee, while the great cats paced up and down with hungry eyes. Marcus kept away from them. The smell of the coming fight was in their nostrils, and they were ready to attack anything. Today they knew they would be well fed.

The area under the arena was like a maze, but Marcus had quickly learned his way around. The tunnels led by steps and slopes up to the gates where the gladiators would enter and through which the chariots would drive. Besides this great entrance, there were many other ways in. Ropes and chains could pull a whole cage up in an instant, so that one moment a tiger could be safely out of sight and the next it would be on the arena floor, ready to attack. Marcus knew that when the hands pulled at the ropes, he would have to get out of the way at just the right moment, or he too would end up as dinner for a hungry cat.

TRAINING THE LIONS

Fully grown lions do not hunt men, so in Roman times they were trained to kill humans. A trainer would slaughter an animal that the lion would eat in the wild, such as a gazelle, and then smear its blood over the body of a man. The smell of the gazelle would confuse the lion, and it would attack the man. After a few times, the lion would attack a man whether he was smeared with animal blood or not.

‖‖‖‖‖‖‖‖‖‖‖‖‖‖‖‖‖‖‖‖‖‖‖‖‖‖‖‖‖

LUCIUS WAS GOING to the barbershop with his father, and they were running late. They must not arrive at the Games after the entrance of the emperor.

Caius went to the same barber every day for a shave, to have his hair trimmed, and to be sprinkled with perfume. And there was the gossip, of course. A senator needed to know what was going on in the city, and where better to learn it than in the easy atmosphere of the barbershop?

Caius had many friends, and they greeted him cheerfully. "So Lucius is shaving now, is he?" shouted fat old Amicus.

Lucius blushed. His father, rather than joining in the laughter, called to the barber, "And take care of my son, please. His beard is coming through, and he needs to look his best. He sits near the emperor today."

The barber recognized the rebuke to Amicus and nodded cautiously. Caius was a powerful man. "Welcome, young Lucius," he said. "So you're going to the Games?"

Lucius was caught between an alarmed sense of his cheeks about to be scraped and pride at his father and with himself. "Oh, yes," he said, as though he sat near the emperor every day in the Colosseum.

"I was sick the first time I went," said an old man with no hair and a beard. Lucius wondered what business he could have in a barbershop, but there was always the perfume and the gossip. The men laughed.

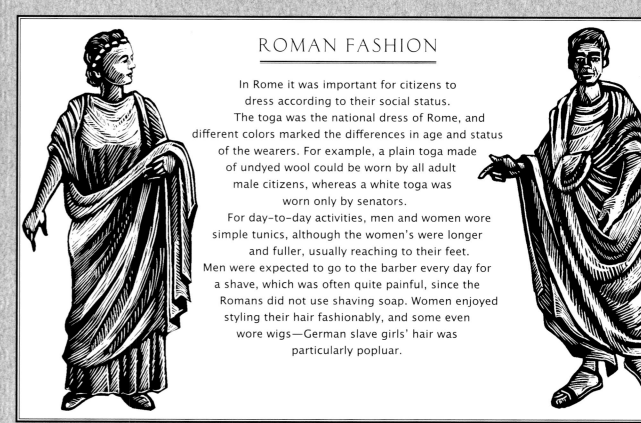

ROMAN FASHION

In Rome it was important for citizens to dress according to their social status. The toga was the national dress of Rome, and different colors marked the differences in age and status of the wearers. For example, a plain toga made of undyed wool could be worn by all adult male citizens, whereas a white toga was worn only by senators. For day-to-day activities, men and women wore simple tunics, although the women's were longer and fuller, usually reaching to their feet. Men were expected to go to the barber every day for a shave, which was often quite painful, since the Romans did not use shaving soap. Women enjoyed styling their hair fashionably, and some even wore wigs—German slave girls' hair was particularly popluar.

MARCUS KNEW THAT THERE WAS one beast that would not be able to enter the arena by being hauled up in a cage. He found escape from the activity and hustle and sought out the elephant, which stood patiently and with a melancholy dignity, unaware of the events about to overtake him. Marcus had felt such awe and longing when he had first seen him in Carthage, where Quintus had bought him. Despite his great size, there was a gentleness and a sadness about him that had drawn Marcus to him. His rough skin and huge careful feet, his small, wise eyes, and his delicate trunk charmed Marcus, who talked to him every day, telling him his fears and longings, things he was too shy even to talk about with Timon.

"You are the greatest beast here," he said softly. "Greater even than the emperor. Come back safely."

⸻

LUCIUS COULD NOT BELIEVE the sight. He had expected the arena to be a vast open space, ready for gladiators to do battle. Instead, it was a park, with trees and plants, paths and open areas. In a short time, the slaves had transformed it by heaving huge amounts of greenery into place, creating the impression of open countryside.

The emperor had made his grand entrance, and Lucius was thrilled to discover that he and his father sat only a few rows away from him. Trajan had even nodded to Caius as he sat down and looked around him.

Almost before Lucius knew what was happening, the gates to the arena were thrust open, and more than a hundred gazelles stormed in, their hooves beating on the hard sand. The boy gasped, entranced by the delicacy and grace of the creatures. The crowd roared its pleasure at the start of the entertainment.

No sooner had the gazelles raced to the other side of the created landscape than twenty wild boars rushed in, followed swiftly by goats, zebras, and a dozen bulls, already crazed with fury from being jabbed with sticks and tormented with flapping cloths.

Far away from Lucius, at the other side of the stadium, money changed hands quickly as bets were placed on which animals would die first.

The boars were the first to kill. Three of them cornered a gazelle and finished it off quickly with their sharp tusks. Lucius did not know where to look: there was so much happening. The peaceful park had become a field of alarm and death.

Marcus felt a different fear as he peered through the gap between the gate and the post. So far, so good. He had kept the gazelles under control right to the last second. The smell of fear was in their nostrils, and they had tried to leap the barriers, but he had calmed them enough to send them running into the arena.

VENATORS

Venators were considered inferior to gladiators, but they still played an important part in the games. They were skilled hunters who relied on their wits and experience to survive the ferocious wild animals they were pitted against. Their task was to stalk and kill the animals, sometimes with their bare hands, but more often with a spear. While it was unusual for a venator to be killed in the hunt, few animals ever left the arena alive.

Just as the crowd began to tire of the scene, the gates swung open again and the venators rushed out, completely unarmed. The crowds loved these contests between man and animal, and the venators were particular favorites. Sometimes the animals had the upper hand, but usually it seemed to be the hunters who were winning. Men and beasts alike were the property of the beast masters, so it didn't really matter who died. In some ways it was better for the men to die. They cost less.

For a while the crowd was entertained by the spectacle, but then they began to grow restless again. The Great Hunt was nearly over, but there was one further thrill to come before the next part of the Games began. Marcus was sweating, not just from the intense heat but from fear and fury. His beloved elephant was the climax of the hunt. He was to enter the arena for the first, and perhaps the last, time.

||||||||||||||||||||||||||||||||

LUCIUS FELT FAINT from the heat, even with the canopy over his head. The noise and excitement of the Games were completely overwhelming to him, but, to his surprise, his father spent much of the time talking to people around him. Lucius couldn't believe it. Here was the most wonderful spectacle, and the men around him were more interested in their conversations than in what they could see.

Then one of them pointed, and the chatter stopped.

"An elephant," said the fat man, Amicus, from the barbershop. "I love to see an elephant."

The huge beast ran delicately into the arena, his trunk aloft, trumpeting the fanfare that had broken Lucius's sleep. Lucius drew in his breath and clenched his fists, delighted at the sight. The whole arena had filled with new animals—antelopes and wild horses, ostriches running frantically in circles, hyenas, and then, to cause more fear and flight, three lionesses.

More venators rode in, this time armed with swords which they slashed from side to side, killing all in their way. The carnivorous animals killed the antelope and gazelles; the hyenas pounced on the dead meat.

Despite all the activity, one sight attracted the most attention—the elephant. At first he ran safely above the fighting, but then two venators drove him to the side of the arena beneath Trajan's seat, while four more made sure that two of the lionesses were driven toward him.

The crowd looked down, anticipating the fall of the magnificent beast. But two pairs of eyes saw differently: Marcus stared in horror as his friend was prepared for the kill, and Lucius, half-crazy with fear for this majestic animal, gazed on in terror.

One of the lionesses was worrying the legs of the elephant, and as he dipped his head to look, the other sprang at his neck, claws gripping the wrinkled skin, teeth seeking flesh to tear open. He turned his head in pain and the other cat leaped up. They had him now, and it was only time before the huge beast would fall, first to his knees, and then to his death.

Lucius could bear it no longer. He stood, turned to the emperor and, looking directly at him, shouted, "Stop them! Make them stop!" Caius grabbed his arm to pull him back to his seat, but Trajan turned his head away from the fight and looked slowly at the boy.

"I am sorry!" said Caius. "Please, it is his first Games."

"Caius," said Trajan, "this is your son?"

"It is."

"Your name, boy."

"Lucius." He could feel the shock of those around him. His father was disgraced. He would be ruined.

"And why should it stop?"

Lucius hung his head.

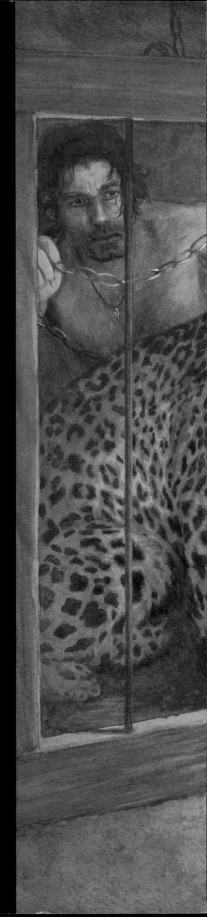

"Answer the emperor," Caius ordered.

"I dreamed of this beast," said Lucius, "and he deserves to live, for . . ." He searched for a reason. "For his dignity."

Amicus laughed. Trajan stared at him, and the fat man fell silent. The emperor looked down. He signaled to the venators, who instantly drove the lionesses from the elephant's neck and shepherded the beast to the gates of the arena.

"Dignity deserves life," said Trajan. "Caius, bring your son to see me soon. I like a Roman citizen who loves life and dignity."

"I will," said Caius.

"And you"—he motioned to a slave who waited near him— "tell the beast master that the elephant belongs to Lucius now." He smiled. "I hope you find room for your prize."

No more words were exchanged that day between Lucius and Trajan. Caius squeezed his son's arm, and they went back to watching the hunt, feeling that some great danger had passed, some great victory had been won.

Below them, the animals were being driven back to the gates, and the scene was changing. Slaves ran on and dragged the trees away, twenty of them straining to move each one. The parkland was disappearing and the clear sand of the arena emerging.

⁕⁕⁕⁕⁕⁕⁕⁕⁕⁕⁕⁕⁕⁕⁕⁕⁕⁕⁕⁕⁕⁕⁕⁕⁕

THE HUNT HAD taken an hour, and Lucius could see the sun high above them, almost at its peak. He felt he'd already seen all the Games had to offer by way of excitement, but there were many more contests to come.

Far beneath Lucius, under the surface of the arena, Marcus was keeping his distance from an angry leopard behind bars. One of the bravest beast fighters had climbed into the cage with a chain around his wrist. While Marcus distracted the leopard, the fighter dropped the looped end of the chain

around the animal's neck. "Go!" he shouted.

The cage was hoisted up, and man and beast sprang into the arena, chained together.

The crowd was on its feet again, cheering. Blinded by the sudden sun, the leopard ran, dragging the man behind him. Then it felt the tug of the chain, and they faced each other. Only one would leave the arena alive.

Within minutes, lions, tigers, and more leopards were driven through the gates or sprang up through the trapdoors. Dogs, working as a pack, harried and hustled a bear. The arena was alive with claws and teeth.

Lucius cheered as the beasts were killed, one by one. Even the man chained to the leopard defeated the cat. As the leopard jumped up to attack, the man turned his weight against it, twisting away and burying a slim dagger deep in its throat till the blood covered his arm and shoulder.

MARCUS CROUCHED in the shadows under the arena, listening to the roar. He'd seen this many times before in many arenas. He felt sick at the sight of these filthy Roman citizens cheering on the slaughter of the wonderful animals he had brought so carefully all the way from Africa. But now the animal fights were over, and a string of men was being led into the arena.

"Who are these people?" Lucius asked. "Are they the gladiators?" That was what he had come for, to see the great fighters.

"Not really," said his father, bored. "These are poor fighters, criminals. None of them will be spared, save perhaps a few who show promise. Time for us to go and eat—leave the rabble to their sport."

The emperor was leaving first. Lucius and Caius waited until he had gone, then they followed him to enjoy a shady meal. But the crowds in the upper tiers were cheering as loudly as ever.

The poor fighters, some of them blindfolded, some still shackled, some armed, others not, fought ferociously against one another, but with little skill or success. They fell one by one to the arena floor.

CRIMINALS

Criminals were executed at lunchtime, a bit like a commercial break between the hunt and the gladiator fights. Executions in the arena were brutal: the unfortunates might face crucifixion, burning, being torn limb from limb by wild animals, or they might be made to fight one another to the death. There was no escape. Any man who fell to the arena floor was prodded with a hot iron by one of the arena slaves. If he moved, another slave would swing a hammer to his head to finish him off. The corpses were dragged off by slaves to be cut up and fed to the animals.

LUCIUS RETURNED TO SEE the last few criminals vainly pleading for mercy. None of them had pleased the crowd enough to be allowed to live, and the people called out for an end to them all.

Just above the shouts of the crowd, Lucius thought he could hear music: lyres and pipes and singing. Slowly the crowd heard it, too, and their shouting died down until the music was clear. The gates were thrown open, and a full-masted sailing ship was wheeled in, crewed by musicians and singers in special Greek costumes. Dancers led them in, and they were followed by scores of people, families of elderly and young, parents and children, fastened together with ropes at the wrist. These prisoners were covered with blue cloth and made to raise and lower their arms, like waves. The dancers climbed aboard the ship, and the

singers sang that land was sighted. The blue cloth was pulled away, and as the ship made safe harbor, all the traps sprang open, the gates burst wide, and the beasts were released, more maddened than ever by the morning's events. They tore into the prisoners, killing for sport, not food, flinging one corpse aside and springing onto another. The dancers and musicians performed above them from the safety of the deck, the singers struggling to be heard over the delighted cheers of the crowd. Even the patricians around the emperor left off their gossip and applauded.

Eventually, the ship disappeared through the gates, and a new sort of chatter began to buzz through the crowd.

"At last," said Caius. "Some sport fit for a Roman."

"At last," said Timon. "Let's show them sport to make me a Roman."

"At last," said Quintus. "I've got enough beasts left to survive another day."

"At last," said Lucius. "Real gladiators."

"At last," said Marcus, stroking the elephant's trunk. "You're safe."

Although the crowds loved seeing the sport with the beasts, everyone loved the gladiators best.

Aquillus, Porcinus, Salvus, Globus, and Timon had all tried to make sure they would not be fighting against one another. All wanted to live to be free men, but none wanted to kill his friend. Instead, they would fight men from other gladiatorial schools.

The crowd cheered as the different gladiators entered the arena, but as soon as Globus walked onto the sand, the loudest cheer of the day went up. He was a special favorite with the crowd.

Globus turned his head to survey the benches, stopping as he faced the emperor, pausing, then giving a slight bow, more a nod of greeting than a sign of respect. The crowd laughed and cheered even louder at this display of arrogance. Trajan's lips nearly lifted in a smile. Globus was like a monument, his huge body even more threatening in the costume of a hoplomachus. In his right hand he wielded a spear, while his left held a small round shield. A helmet and shoulder guard finished the armor. Timon and the others looked like fighting men, but Globus was the image of a god come to life.

The contests began with Timon the first among his friends up at combat. He dispatched his first opponent so quickly and with so much ease that the crowd booed him.

"Why are they booing?" asked Lucius.

"They think it was too easy," said Caius. "It was not a contest. But that one is good, you see."

So Lucius kept an eye on Timon and saw that his father was right. He won every contest, but never so easily as the first.

"See?" said Caius. "He has learned not to win too soon."

Lucius also saw that once Timon rescued another fighter without seeming to do so.

After half an hour, only the better fighters were left. The five friends from the school of Quintus kept well away from one another, anxious not to be drawn into doing battle together.

Aquillus and Porcinus attracted much admiration for the spectacular way they threw their nets and then pounced to finish off their opponents with their tridents. And while the aristocrats enjoyed the skill and professionalism of Timon, it was Globus who once again stole the show. He stood, massive and confident, right in the center of the arena, half facing the emperor's box and taking on all opponents. His upper body was drenched in his own blood and the blood of those he had killed. But his wounds were light and would soon heal, unlike the fatal thrusts he made into others.

Bets were being made on the different gladiators, and a rumble ran through the crowd; Timon's supporters thought he could beat Globus, and Globus's fans wanted to put their money on him against Timon.

A roar went up for the two champions to fight against each other.

Aquillus and Porcinus had survived. They would fight another day. Raising their weapons first to their comrades, then to the crowd, they left the arena. Salvus, despite Timon's saving his life in the arena once that day, had not been so lucky. Only Globus and Timon remained on the floor.

‖‖‖‖‖‖‖‖‖‖‖‖‖‖‖‖‖‖‖‖‖‖‖‖‖

MARCUS WATCHED from a high vantage point. He had left the dank and stinking pits where the slaughtered animals and butchered men had been dragged, and he now made his way to a place where he could see without interruption. Quintus would be pleased. The Games were a great success and his animals and gladiators were performing well. Marcus watched as Globus and Timon sized each other up. The swift skill of the mirmillo was pitted against the weight and strength of the hoplomachus. Marcus felt sick with fear as he saw Timon, who was all he had for a father, face Globus, the killing machine.

‖‖‖‖‖‖‖‖‖‖‖‖‖‖‖‖‖‖‖‖‖‖‖‖‖‖‖

"I BET ON THE FAT ONE," said Amicus.

"That's Globus," said Lucius, who had studied the names.

"And I bet on the other one," said Caius.

"That's Timon," said Lucius, who thought his father was making a mistake. The big one would win. And anyway, Lucius preferred Globus, who made the crowd laugh as he fought and cheer as he killed. Timon was a serious fighter, not a showman.

"I bet on Globus as well," said Lucius. "He's more like a Roman."

"How so?" asked his father.

"Strong, brave, and nothing stops him. He is like a legion all on his own."

"Good," said Amicus. "The Roman legion is unstoppable."

"Ah," said Caius, "but look at the other. He moves sideways when he needs to and takes fewer wounds. He knows when to strike, when to dodge, and when to kill. The fat one wastes energy by standing still and defending himself. My man thinks about the fight, and though he seems to do less, he lets his enemies defeat themselves by watching for their weaknesses. It is brains and skill that have made Rome great, not just brute force."

"But think of the legions," said Amicus.

It was Timon who struck the first blow and Timon who dodged so that Globus could not strike back. The second and third blows were his, too, and though Globus parried them with his shield, they were well aimed and strong and jarred his shoulder, unbalancing him.

Globus struck next, right in the center of Timon's shield, driving him back and unsettling him, so that he stumbled and fell to one knee. Globus, never slow to scent an opportunity, rushed forward to finish it off, but Timon twisted and Globus missed, driving his spear into the sand. They both found their feet again and squared up.

The other fights had gone on in a muddle of bodies. This was the first to capture the attention of the entire crowd on its own. For the first time, Lucius realized he was watching two men trying to kill each other. They were people, not just fighters. He could see the expressions on their faces, feel the need to survive. When Globus thrust his spear into Timon's thigh, Lucius winced with pain. He stood and made his way toward the exit. Casting a glance over his shoulder, he saw Globus towering over Timon, spear upraised for the kill. The roar of the crowd nearly made Lucius faint, and he turned away and ran.

Lucius ran out of the Games like a frightened slave. He ran and ran and didn't stop until he reached the open countryside. He flung himself down on the hard ground and sat with his back to the Colosseum, the sound of cheering still in his head.

Lucius was ashamed of himself. And yet he was glad he had not seen the man killed. There was something about Timon that made him seem nobler than many of the citizens who lined up every morning to beg favors from his father. Lucius couldn't make sense of it. He sat for some time until he knew he would have to go back.

Exhausted and confused, he stood up, turned his face back to Rome, and started to walk toward his home.

|||||||||||||||||||||||||||||||||

MARCUS CAME UP and looked around at the empty arena. Now the sun was low in the sky, and the crowds had all left. In the maze of passageways beneath him, food sellers, traders, beast masters, and gladiators thronged the labyrinth, and the traders struggled to be heard above the noises of the animals being driven back into the cages.

Quintus had been bad-tempered after the fight. He had found Marcus feeding the elephant, holding a bucket of water for the animal to spray into his mouth. Quintus had ordered Marcus out of the Colosseum to find him something to eat.

"I won't eat the filth they sell here," he had said crossly.

Marcus had left quickly. He had to trot behind a winding procession of carts piled with carcasses to get away from the Colosseum. The bodies stank in the heat, and the slaves worked tirelessly to get rid of the dead before they could cause a public nuisance. Some were taken to deep, wide graves that had been prepared earlier, others to the Tiber, the river that ran through Rome, where they were tipped into the sluggish water till it ran red with blood.

Marcus watched as the carts were tilted and the bodies slid off. He tried not to think about the friend he had lost in the arena today.

〰️〰️〰️〰️〰️〰️〰️〰️

LUCIUS WOULD BE IN TROUBLE. It was too late for him to be out alone, but he could not believe the sights before him. His father's house was in the rich part of the city. He had never seen this side of Rome, at night after the Games. The mass of bodies and carcasses sickened him. All the excitement of the day, which had been played out below him by figures who had seemed no more real than toy soldiers, now lay before him as a horror of broken bodies.

The carts trundled their bloody burdens to the river, arms and legs hanging from the sides, heads lolling lifelessly. Lucius didn't want to look at them, but he couldn't turn his eyes away, either. He had cheered as these men had killed one another.

There was no point in going home to sleep. He would only dream of their dead faces. So he walked, tired yet determined, not knowing where he was going, until he realized he was utterly lost.

Just as Lucius was about to despair, he saw a face he recognized in the crowd: the boy who had stolen his food hours ago, who had shamed him in front of the stallkeeper. He was still carrying food—surely not the same pastries!

Lucius followed him, curious to see where he was going. Perhaps he would lead him to a place he would recognize.

|||||||||||||||||||||||||||||||||||

QUINTUS FINISHED HIS CALCULATIONS. Despite his grumpy expression, he was more than pleased with the day. He had lost more than half of his animals and the elephant as well. Thirty-one slaves had been killed and three top gladiators lost: Salvus, Globus, and Timon. But the payment was more than enough to make up for the losses. He had already bought from another beast master nearly twenty wounded slaves who could be patched up. Now he wanted to return to Africa as soon as he could to gather a new menagerie of animals.

Scraps of food clung to his beard as he looked at Marcus with a friendly eye. "You do good work, boy," he said, and he tossed him a couple of silver coins. "You'd better say good-bye to your elephant."

Lucius observed what was happening from behind a pillar. He did not know why he had followed this boy. It was not to fight with him again. Even if he had wanted to, he doubted it would be wise. There seemed to be no law here, no order that came from the empire. This space underneath the Colosseum was a world on its own, and the boy was more a citizen here than Lucius was. So he trailed him as he went through the tunnels, attending to the beasts, chattering to the gladiators, and pilfering food from the stalls.

They seemed to be going deeper into the labyrinth, and the boy darted so much that Lucius nearly lost him several times. Then, after the boy had taken three left turns in a row at a fair pace, Lucius found himself in a deserted area with all noise far behind him, looking at an empty passageway. The boy had disappeared, and Lucius had completely lost his way. Wishing that he hadn't followed him, Lucius decided to try the path to his left. Before he had gone three paces, the slave boy stepped out from the shadows.

"Why are you following me?"

The darkness was not deep enough to hide the alarm on Lucius' face, nor to disguise him from Marcus.

"You were in the food market today."

Lucius nodded.

"Have you come to have me arrested?" Marcus advanced, his hands clenched.

"No."

"Why are you here? You don't belong here."

In a sudden inspiration, Lucius said, "The emperor gave me an elephant. I'm here to take it."

Marcus laughed. "You!" But his scorn was mixed with anger and sorrow. If anyone should take his friend, it should not be this arrogant Roman boy.

"That's right."

"I could kill you here," said Marcus. "No one would ever know. Kill you and toss you on the cart. Does your mother know you're out?"

"My father is just behind me," said Lucius. "We parted a few minutes ago."

"Liar. I've watched you since the road. You're alone. Did you enjoy the Games? Did you like seeing the men die? One more boy won't matter."

"One more boy?" said a deep voice.

Lucius turned to see Globus, the huge hoplomachus from the last fight of the afternoon. He was bandaged where he had been wounded, but he walked steadily. Lucius gasped in terror. He knew that he was about to die.

"One more boy," Globus said again. "Don't you think there have been enough deaths today, Marcus?"

As Marcus and Globus faced each other, Lucius found new courage.

"Take this boy away," he ordered Globus. "Take him to the magistrate and deal with him. Do as I say."

Globus turned to Lucius, looking menacing.

WINNING FREEDOM

Gladiators were slaves, owned and kept by their masters. Because of this, they could only be rewarded with freedom in response to the wishes of the crowd. It was a rare sight, since the owner of the gladiator would lose a valuable slave who earned him a lot of money. A wooden sword was presented as the symbol of freedom and after that the gladiator was free from any obligation to fight again. However, some gladiators chose to remain as fighters. The most famous was called Flamma, who was eventually killed in his 34th fight, having been offered his freedom on four separate occasions.

"Mind your manners, boy."

"How dare you speak to a Roman citizen like that," said Lucius.

Globus smiled. Lucius felt more fear than ever. "And how dare you speak to me like that," said Globus. "I think you'd better follow me."

So the emperor had made Globus a free man.

Lucius had no choice but to follow, although he resented walking behind Globus and alongside Marcus. He kept his distance from both of them.

They were soon back in the throng of activity, and before Lucius knew it, the elephant stood before him. Quintus was untying him.

"That's mine?" he said to Globus.

Globus nodded. "I've brought you here to take it."

"Why is it his? He has no right!" Marcus was furious.

"He saved the beast's life," said Quintus. "You were busy with the cages. This boy begged the mercy of the emperor and was rewarded."

Marcus struggled with his feelings. He hated the boy, yet Lucius had saved his friend the elephant.

"It was a good day for granting mercy," said Globus. "Or I should be dead."

"I've never heard of a day like it before," said Timon, walking toward them out of the shadows. "The emperor has never saved both men in a fight to the death." He put his hand on Globus's shoulder.

"It was the crowd," said Marcus. "They gave you life."

"And freedom," Timon reminded him.

"Only the emperor can do that," said Lucius. "You don't understand."

"Don't I, little Roman?" Globus said. "Listen. Every emperor rules by the consent of the people. Take away that consent, and he will fall. It was the crowd. They were evenly matched in support of us. If the emperor had ordered the death of either one of us, there would have been riots tonight, and when order breaks down, it is hard to restore. Even in Rome."

"What will you do now?" asked Lucius.

"Me?" said Globus. "No more fighting. I'll start my own school for gladiators. Watch others die."

"Me?" said Timon. "Home. No more Rome. No more fighting, even in war. I will buy a farm and live in peace."

"Me?" said Quintus. "Back to Africa to find more animals for the hunt."

Lucius looked at Marcus, who had remained silent.

"I belong to him," he said, nodding toward Quintus. "Back to Africa for me, too. Till I am old enough to fight and become a free man."

Lucius felt the sadness of this reply, more than he saw it in Marcus's face.

"No," said Quintus. "You're no good to me. Not without Timon. You'll just mope. You'd better go with him. I give you to him. Get out of my sight."

Marcus stared.

"And I give you to yourself," said Timon.

Quintus looked away, but Marcus ran over and hugged him.

"Go away," said Quintus. "And give this young man his elephant."

LUCIUS THOUGHT THAT HE would be in trouble in the morning but that perhaps the carnival atmosphere of the day would save him. He stared out of his window into the midnight sky. The gardens of the villa swept out below him. They looked big enough for an elephant. Perhaps he should have kept it.

IN THE FIELDS OUTSIDE THE CITY, Timon and Marcus looked up at the stars. The elephant grazed noisily.

"Are you sure you can keep an elephant on a farm?" asked Marcus.

"Easily."

"How will we get him there, though?"

"Slowly."

They laughed, disturbing the beast, who raised his trunk into the air and trumpeted a victory fanfare, breaking into the dreams of the distant Lucius, who smiled and turned, then drifted once more into peaceful slumber.

Roman Emperors to AD 192

Augustus	27 BC–AD 14
Tiberius	14–37
Gaius (Caligula)	37–41
Claudius	41–54
Nero	54–68
Galba	68–69
Otho	69
Vitellius	69
Vespasian	69–79
Titus	79–81
Domitian	81–96
Nerva	96–98
Trajan	98–117
Hadrian	117–138
Antoninus Pius	138–161
Marcus Aurelius	161–180
Lucius Verus (co-emperor with M. Aurelius)	161–169
Commodus	180–192

Text copyright © 2009 by Toby Forward

Illustrations copyright © 2009 by Steve Noon

Black and white illustrations © 2009 by Brian@KJA-artists.com

First U.S. edition 2009

Library of Congress Cataloging-in-Publication Data is available.

Library of Congress Catalog Card Number 2009921773

ISBN 978-0-7636-4444-4

2 4 6 8 10 9 7 5 3 1

Printed in China

This book was typeset in Lucida.

The illustrations were done in watercolor and ink.

Candlewick Press, 99 Dover Street, Somerville, Massachusetts 02144

visit us at www.candlewick.com